I'm Just Like My Grandma
I'm Just Like My Grandpa

Create the connection that lasts forever.

Vickie Mullins

Azure Eyes Publishing
Scottsdale, Arizona

www.imjustlikemy.com

 I'm Just Like My ...

Copyright © 2005 Vickie Mullins

All rights reserved. Printed in the United States of America. No part of this publication may be reproduced, stored in a retrieval system or transmitted in any form or by any means, electronic, mechanical, photocopying, recording or otherwise, without the written permission of the publisher. General references to the book name and type or brief quotation in printed reviews are an exception.

Published by
Azure Eyes Publishing
7520 E. Second Street, Ste. 5
Scottsdale, AZ 85251

www.imjustlikemy.com

Quotes copyright, "Worth Repeating: More than 5,000 Classic and Contemporary Quotes" by Bob Kelly

This book is a non-fiction work. Any personal reference to actual people is with permission.

Second Edition—October 2005

ISBN 0-9769923-0-2

Create the connection that lasts forever.

This book
is dedicated to the memory of
Shelly Reklaitis

❤ How this book came to be ...

In January of 2004, Shelly Reklaitis was diagnosed with six brain tumors, melanoma that had metastasized eight years after having skin cancer removed from her leg. A devoted young mother of four children under the age of six—Mykol, Elizabeth, Viktoria and Kristina—Shelly was given a life expectancy of about six months.

I had become acquainted with Shelly through her husband Paul, a business associate and friend. Like so many people who knew the family, I struggled with what I could do to help the Reklaitis family as their lives quickly unraveled.

Out of my frustration to create a contribution to Shelly's comfort, I put myself in Shelly's place and thought of what I might want. It was immediately obvious; I would want my children to know ME as a person, the person who will always be their mom. I would want them to feel connected to me even though I was no longer a part of their daily lives and their memories faded. That although I was absent, I could always be a part of them because they could connect so many likenesses we shared.

continued

The Reklaitis Family

Create the connection that lasts forever.

Shelly found comfort in my idea, so she and Paul answered my questions. Then, we set the answers aside. Shelly died August 6, 2004. Her life was the inspiration of *I'm Just Like My ...*, and she is the spiritual author of this project.

Moving from sadness to celebration of life lived well, as every family participates in their own "collection of answers," a connection is made with Shelly and her family. A heightened sense of relationship becomes possible.

Each family can appreciate what is happening today, share themselves with loved ones and create comfort for their families as they move into the future.

Welcome to the circle you just joined as you participate in your copy of *I'm Just Like My ...*

vm

❤ Acknowledgements

I'm Just Like My ... was not planned by anyone on this earth, but I believe God, in His infinite wisdom planned it long ago. As I look back over my life, I can see where He led me to get the experience and learn the lessons I would need to be able to complete this project. It is not my idea, it is His. He placed the passion so deep in my heart, that I had no choice but to do it. Then He surrounded me with everyone I needed to accomplish the task at hand.

I express my gracious thanks to my La Casa de Cristo friends who listened, believed in me and kept the encouragement coming.

I would like to acknowledge Michelle Cubas who saw the vision, embraced it and served as the mid-wife bringing this project to life.

A special thank you to Tom Howard and Brandi Hollister for contributing their incredible design talents to turn the idea into a visual reality.

Thank you to Paul Reklaitis for allowing me in to his family's life as it turned upside down. Your trust and openness enabled Shelly's legacy to live on.

Special thanks to my husband Jack; he has always been there for me, patiently listening as I unloaded another idea on him. Jack's the one who has always given me the support and confidence to tackle anything.

To my children – Jonathan and Shannon – you are just like Dad, you are just like me, you make everything worthwhile.

 I'm Just Like My ...

Create the connection that lasts forever.

Author Vickie Mullins invites you to embark on a journey. Along your pathway you can enjoy sharing, reflecting, giving and contributing from the fabric of your life to that of the entire family.

With the frenetic pace of today's lifestyles, sometimes we forget to connect to the greatest source of happiness and energy we will ever know. Whether you're on the phone with your relatives or live together, *I'm Just Like My ...* makes it easy to connect with your family, both geographically and psychologically.

Vickie challenges us to consider what we want people to remember about us. This isn't mournful. It is a sacred trust and a fragile one, because once the thread is broken, it is nearly impossible to recapture an actual connection to a loved one.

There is a saying, "Everyone has at least one book inside them." This is your moment. Make it happen for you and your family. Enjoy the journey.

You are about to begin the Grandma's section of *I'm Just Like My ...* To complete Grandpa's connection, turn to page 71.

❤ How to Use This Book

Find yourself a comfortable chair and get ready to have some fun. Here are a few ways this book can be utilized.

1. As a tool to initiate a family dialogue.

Even the closest families most likely haven't shared the answers to many of the questions contained within these covers. Gather your loved ones around a table and let the conversations begin. The extra lines below each question will allow for multiple entries.

2. As a personal legacy for later review.

Life is unpredictable, none of us knows for sure what the future holds. By taking the time now to record this information, those who are left behind after a loved one's passing will have everything they need to know to make a heart-to-heart connection that will last forever. It is a precious gift of oneself that cannot be replaced.

3. As an opportunity to personally reach out to touch one specific person.

Families will find this book a valuable resource to bring loved ones back home emotionally. It is a non-threatening opportunity to show individuality as a person as well as the traits that make each person part of something larger than themselves.

Regardless of how you choose to use this book, I encourage you to be generous with the information you provide; the more you share, the stronger your connection can be.

vm

www.ImJustLikeMy.com

I'm Just Like My Grandma

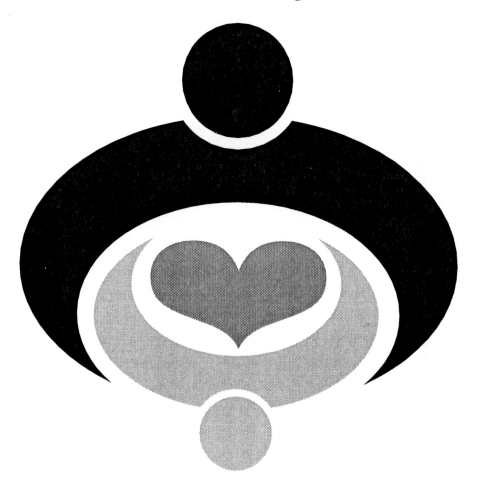

Create the connection that lasts forever.

 I'm Just Like My ... Grandma

This book is about making a connection to:

_____
(Grandma, write your name here)

Section One

❤ physical characteristics

❤ **What color is your hair?**

....

....

....

....

....

....

....

I'm Just Like My ... Grandma

The average person has 100,000 hairs on his/her head.

❤ Is your hair thick or thin?

....
....
....
....
....
....
....

❤ Do you have a widow's peak?

....
....
....
....
....
....

❤ Where does your hair part naturally, on the left, center or right?

....
....
....
....
....
....

❤ Is your hair curly or straight?

....
....
....
....
....
....

My mom always told me, "Eat the crusts on your bread or your curls will go away."

Create the connection that lasts forever.

❤ **Do you have any cowlicks?**

....

....

....

....

....

....

....

❤ **Are your earlobes attached at the base?**

....

....

....

....

....

....

....

❤ **Do your ears stick out or do they lay flat?**

....
....
....
....
....
....
....

The one who listens is the one who understands.
~ African Proverb

❤ **Are your ears pierced?**

....
....
....
....
....
....
....

If your ears are pierced, how many piercings do you hove in each ear?

....
....
....

Create the connection that lasts forever.

I'm Just Like My ... Grandma

Family faces are magic mirrors. Looking at people who belong to us, we see the past, present and future. We make discoveries about ourselves.

~ Gail Lumen Buckle

❤ **Is your face round, oval or square?**

....
....
....
....
....
....
....

❤ **Do you have high cheek bones?**

....
....
....
....
....
....

❤ **Do you have a large or small forehead?**

....
....
....
....
....
....
....

❤ **Do you have dimples?**

.... If you do have dimples, where are they?

....

....

....

....

....

Create the connection that lasts forever.

I'm Just Like My ... Grandma

Some people believe freckles are left from kisses by angels.

❤ **Do you have any freckles?**

....
....
....
....
....
....
....

❤ **What color are your eyes?**

....
....
....
....
....
....

❤ **What shape are your eyes?**

....

....

....

....

....

....

....

Our eyes remain the same size from birth.

❤ **Do you wear contacts, eyeglasses or neither?**

....

....

....

....

....

....

If you wear contacts or glasses, are you far-sighted or near-sighted?

....

....

....

Create the connection that lasts forever.

I'm Just Like My ... Grandma

Your nose and ears never stop growing.

❤ Is your nose big or small?

....
....
....
....
....
....
....

❤ Is your nose pointy or rounded?

....
....
....
....
....
....
....

♥ **Are your lips thin or full?**

....
....
....
....
....
....
....

♥ **Are your teeth naturally crooked or straight?**

	Did you ever wear braces on your teeth?
....	
....	....
....	
....	....
....	
....	....
	At what age?
....	....

Create the connection that lasts forever.

I'm Just Like My ... Grandma

❤ **Do you have a cleft chin?**

....

....

....

....

....

....

❤ **Is your chin pointed or round?**

....

....

....

....

....

....

♥ **Do you have a unibrow?**

....
....
....
....
....
....
....

♥ **Do you have long or short eyelashes?**

....
....
....
....
....
....
....

Create the connection that lasts forever.

I'm Just Like My ... Grandma

A smile is the shortest distance between two people.
~ Victor Borge

❤ **Do you squint when you smile?**

....
....
....
....
....
....
....

❤ **Are you big-boned or petite?**

....
....
....
....
....
....

❤ **Do you have thick or thin ankles?**

....
....
....
....
....
....
....

❤ **Do you have thick or thin wrists?**

....
....
....
....
....
....

Create the connection that lasts forever.

I'm Just Like My ... Grandma

❤ How tall are you?

....
....
....
....
....
....
....

❤ Do you have long legs or short legs?

....
....
....
....
....
....
....

❤ Do you have lots of hair on your body or just a little?

....
....
....
....
....
....

Men lose about 40 hairs a day. Women lose about 70 hairs a day.

❤ Are you high-waisted or low-waisted?

....
....
....
....
....
....

Create the connection that lasts forever.

❤ **Do you have an "inny" or "outy" belly button?**

....
....
....
....
....
....

❤ **Do you have a long or short trunk?**

....
....
....
....
....
....

♥ Are your arms long, short or medium?

....

....

....

....

....

....

....

♥ Do you cross your arms right-over-left or left-over-right?

....

....

....

....

....

....

Create the connection that lasts forever.

I'm Just Like My ... Grandma

❤ **What is your ring size?**

....
....
....
....
....
....
....

❤ **Are you allergic to anything?**

....
....
....
....
....
....

The following eight foods account for 90% of all food-allergic reactions: milk, egg, peanut and tree nuts (walnut, cashew, etc.), fish, shellfish, soy and wheat.

❤ **Are you coordinated or clumsy?**

....

....

....

....

....

....

....

❤ **Is your skin smooth or rough?**

....

....

....

....

....

....

....

❤ Are your fingers and toes long or short?

....

....

....

....

....

....

....

❤ Do you have straight or curved thumbs?

....

....

....

....

....

....

❤ **Are your fingernails strong or weak?**

....

....

....

....

....

....

....

❤ **Do you bite your fingernails?**

....

....

....

....

....

....

....

Fingernails grow nearly 4 times faster than toenails.

Create the connection that lasts forever.

I'm Just Like My ... Grandma

> God has given us two hands — one to receive with and the other to give with.
>
> ~ Billy Graham

❤ **Are you right handed or left handed?**

....

....

....

....

....

....

....

❤ **Are your second toes longer than your big toes?**

....

....

....

....

....

❤ What is your shoe size?

....

....

....

....

....

....

....

❤ Are your feet wide or narrow?

....

....

....

....

....

....

Create the connection that lasts forever.

I'm Just Like My ... Grandma

❤ **Do you have a deep voice or a high voice?**

....
....
....
....
....
....
....

❤ **Can you sing well?**

....
....
....
....
....
....

A friend hears the song of the heart and sings it when memory fails.

~ Martin Luther

♥ **Can you whistle with just your lips?**

....

....

....

....

....

....

....

♥ **Can you whistle using your fingers?**

....

....

....

....

....

....

....

Create the connection that lasts forever.

I'm Just Like My ... Grandma

❤ **Can you roll your Rs?**

....

....

....

....

....

....

❤ **Can you touch your tongue to your nose?**

....

....

....

....

....

....

Your tongue is the strongest muscle in your body.

❤ **Can you roll your tongue?**

....
....
....
....
....
....
....

Or are you even more special and have the ability to turn it into a "w"?

....

❤ **Can you wiggle your ears?**

....
....
....
....
....
....

Create the connection that lasts forever.

I'm Just Like My ... Grandma

❤ **Can you wiggle your nose?**

....
....
....
....
....
....
....

❤ **Can you flare your nostrils?**

....
....
....
....
....
....

❤ Can you blow a bubble with gum?

....
....
....
....
....
....
....

According to Guinness World Records, the greatest diameter for a bubble gum bubble is 23".

❤ Do you have a unique physical characteristic?

....
....
....
....
....
....

Create the connection that lasts forever.

❤ Are you limber or stiff?

....
....
....
....
....
....
....

❤ Have you ever been able to do a cartwheel?

....
....
....
....
....
....
....

❤ **Have you ever been able to do a hand stand?**

....
....
....
....
....
....

❤ **Can you bend over and touch your toes?**

....
....
....
....
....
....

Create the connection that lasts forever.　**35**

❤ Do you sunburn or go directly to tan?

....
....
....
....
....
....

❤ What is your blood type?

....
....
....
....
....
....
....

Section Two

❤ personal details & preferences

❤ Are you energetic or calm?

....

....

....

....

....

....

....

Create the connection that lasts forever.

I'm Just Like My ... Grandma

❤ **Are you a morning person or a night owl?**

....

....

....

....

....

....

....

I have never known an early riser to be compelled to hurry.
~ J.B. Chapman

❤ **What is your favorite sleeping position?**

....

....

....

....

....

....

Only humans sleep on their backs.

❤ **What do you wear to sleep in?**

....

....

....

....

....

....

....

❤ **Are you a deep sleeper or a light sleeper?**

....

....

....

....

....

....

Did you know that on average, a person spends about 122 days a year sleeping?

I'm Just Like My ... Grandma

Are your pillows soft or hard?

....

....

....

❤ Do you sleep with one pillow or multiple pillows?

....

....

....

....

....

....

❤ Do you like a soft or hard mattress?

....

....

....

....

....

....

❤ **Do you fall asleep when your head hits the pillow or does it take awhile to doze off?**

....

....

....

....

....

....

The average person falls asleep in seven minutes.

❤ **Do you like to sleep in a cold room with lots of covers or a warm room with few covers?**

....

....

....

....

....

Create the connection that lasts forever.

I'm Just Like My ... Grandma

Scientists have found that it is impossible to tickle yourself. A region in the posterior portion of the brain warns the rest of your brain when you are attempting to tickle yourself.

❤ **Where are you ticklish?**

....
....
....
....
....
....
....

❤ **Are you a leader or a follower?**

....
....
....
....
....
....
....

❤ Do you have a nervous habit?

....

....

....

....

....

....

....

❤ What makes you laugh?

....

....

....

....

....

....

....

The most completely lost of all days is the one on which we have not laughed.

~ Anonymous

Create the connection that lasts forever.

I'm Just Like My ... Grandma

❤ Are you a good speller?

....
....
....
....
....
....
....

❤ Do you prefer baths or showers?

....
....
....
....
....
....

Water consumption averages 7-10 gallons for showers, baths average 20 gallons.

❤ **What makes you cry?**

....

....

....

....

....

....

....

Tears are the safety valve of the heart when too much pressure is laid on.

~ Albert Smith

❤ **Are you messy or neat?**

....

....

....

....

....

....

....

I'm Just Like My ... Grandma

❤ **What are you afraid of?**

....
....
....
....
....
....

Nothing in life is to be feared. It is only to be understood.

~ Marie Curie

❤ **What leg do you put into your pants first?**

....
....
....
....
....
....

❤ **What type of music do you prefer?**

....

....

....

....

....

....

....

My heart, which is full to overflowing, has often been solaced and refreshed by music when sick and weary.
~ Martin Luther

❤ **Do you prefer the mountains or the beach?**

....

....

....

....

....

....

....

Create the connection that lasts forever.

I'm Just Like My ... Grandma

According to Crayola®, America's favorite crayon color is blue.

❤ **What is your favorite color?**

....

....

....

....

....

....

....

❤ **What is your favorite holiday?**

....

....

....

....

....

....

❤ **What is your favorite weather?**

....

....

....

....

....

....

....

❤ **Do you have a favorite pet?**

....

....

....

....

....

....

No symphony orchestra ever played music like a two-year-old girl laughing with a puppy.
~ Bern Williams

Create the connection that lasts forever.

I'm Just Like My ... Grandma

❤ **What is your favorite wild animal?**

....

....

....

....

....

....

❤ **What is your favorite smell?**

How about bread baking or line-dried cotton sheets or fresh cut grass or pine trees or the smell after a rain or ...

....

....

....

....

....

....

❤ Are you an outdoor or an indoor person?

....
....
....
....
....
....
....

❤ What is your favorite season?

....
....
....
....
....
....

Create the connection that lasts forever.

I'm Just Like My ... Grandma

❤ **Would you rather vacation in a tent or a hotel?**

....

....

....

....

....

....

❤ **What is your favorite flower?**

....

....

....

....

....

....

God gave us our memories so we might have roses in December.

~ James. M. Barrie

❤ Do you prefer briefs, bikinis or thongs?

....

....

....

....

....

....

....

❤ Do you like surprises?

....

....

....

....

....

....

Create the connection that lasts forever.

♥ **Can you keep a secret?**

....

....

....

....

....

....

....

♥ **Do you like being alone or with a group?**

....

....

....

....

....

....

....

❤ **Is your glass half empty or half full?**

....
....
....
....
....
....
....

❤ **Are you shy or outgoing?**

....
....
....
....
....
....
....

Create the connection that lasts forever.

I'm Just Like My ... Grandma

❤ **What kinds of snacks do you like?**

....

....

....

....

....

....

❤ **What is your favorite hot beverage?**

....

....

....

....

....

....

❤ What is your favorite cold beverage?

....

....

....

....

....

....

....

❤ Is your favorite meal breakfast, lunch or dinner?

....

....

....

....

....

The first thing I remember liking that liked me back was food.

~ Rhoda Morgenstern

Create the connection that lasts forever.

I'm Just Like My ... Grandma

❤ **What do you like on your hamburgers?**

....

....

....

....

....

....

....

❤ **What is your favorite fruit?**

....

....

....

....

....

....

❤ **What is your favorite vegetable?**

....
....
....
....
....
....
....

❤ **What is your least favorite food?**

....
....
....
....
....
....

If you think advertising doesn't work, consider the millions of Americans who now think that yogurt tastes good.

~ Joe L. Whitley

Create the connection that lasts forever.

I'm Just Like My ... Grandma

❤ **Do you like food hot & spicy or mild?**

....
....
....
....
....
....
....

❤ **What do you like on your pizza?**

....
....
....
....
....
....

Americans, on the average, eat 18 acres of pizza every day.

❤ What is your favorite ice cream topping?

....

....

....

....

....

....

....

❤ What is your favorite sport to watch?

....

....

....

....

....

....

....

I'm Just Like My ... Grandma

Sports do not build character. They reveal it.

~ Heywood Broun

♥ **What is your favorite sport to play?**

....

....

....

....

....

....

....

♥ **Do you like to read?**

....

If you like to read, what types of books do you prefer?

....

....

....

....

....

....

....

....

❤ **Are you creative or analytical?**

....
....
....
....
....
....
....

❤ **Can you swim?**

....
....
....
....
....
....

Create the connection that lasts forever.

I'm Just Like My ... Grandma

❤ Have you ever done a flip off a diving board?

....
....
....
....
....
....

❤ Have you ever been able to do the splits?

....
....
....
....
....
....

❤ **Can you play a musical instrument?**

....

....

....

....

....

....

....

If so, did you ever take lessons on this instrument?

....

....

....

And for how long?

....

❤ **What was your favorite subject in school?**

....

....

....

....

....

....

....

School is a building that has four walls— with tomorrow inside.
~ Lon Watters

Create the connection that lasts forever.

I'm Just Like My ... Grandma

If you're in-between, where are you in the order?

....

....

....

❤ **In your family, are you the oldest, youngest, middle, in-between, or only child?**

....

....

....

....

....

....

❤ **Do you remember other people's names or faces best?**

....

....

....

....

....

❤ **Do you talk to yourself out loud?**

....

....

....

....

....

....

....

❤ Use this space for anything else you may want to share.

I'm Just Like My ...

I'm Just Like My Grandpa

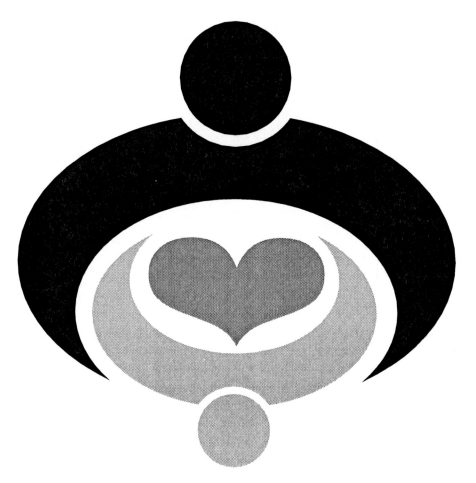

Create the connection that lasts forever.

I'm Just Like My ... Grandpa

This book is about making a connection to:

_____
(Grandpa, write your name here)

Section One

♥ physical characteristics

♥ What color is your hair?

....

....

....

....

....

....

....

Create the connection that lasts forever.

I'm Just Like My ... Grandpa

❤ **Is your hair thick or thin?**

....
....
....
....
....
....
....

❤ **Is your hair curly or straight?**

....
....
....
....
....
....
....

❤ Where does your hair part naturally, on the left, center or right?

....
....
....
....
....
....

❤ Are you balding?

....
....
....
....
....
....

The average person has 100,000 hairs on his/her head.

Create the connection that lasts forever.

❤ **Do you have any cowlicks?**

....

....

....

....

....

....

❤ **Are your earlobes attached at the base?**

....

....

....

....

....

....

❤ **Do your ears stick out or do they lay flat?**

....

....

....

....

....

....

....

Listen, or thy tongue will keep thee deaf.

~ Native American Proverb

❤ **Are your ears pierced?**

....

....

....

....

....

....

Create the connection that lasts forever.

I'm Just Like My ... Grandpa

❤ Is your face round, oval or square?

....
....
....
....
....
....
....

❤ Do you have a large or small Adam's apple?

....
....
....
....
....
....
....

❤ **Do you have a large or small forehead?**

....
....
....
....
....
....
....

❤ **Do you have dimples?**

	If you do have dimples, where are they?
....	
....	....
....	
....	....
....	
....	....
....	

Create the connection that lasts forever.

I'm Just Like My ... Grandpa

Some people believe freckles are left from kisses by angels.

❤ **Do you have any freckles?**

....
....
....
....
....
....
....

❤ **What color are your eyes?**

....
....
....
....
....
....

❤ **What shape are your eyes?**

....

....

....

....

....

....

....

Our eyes remain the same size from birth.

❤ **Do you wear contacts, eyeglasses or neither?**

....

....

....

....

....

....

If you wear contacts or glasses, are you far-sighted or near-sighted?

....

....

....

Create the connection that lasts forever.

I'm Just Like My ... Grandpa

❤ Is your nose pointy or rounded?

....

....

....

....

....

....

....

❤ Is your nose big or small?

....

....

....

....

....

....

❤ **Are your lips thin or full?**

....
....
....
....
....
....
....

❤ **Are your teeth naturally crooked or straight?**

	Did you ever wear braces on your teeth?
....	
....	....
....	....
....	....
....	At what age?
....	....

Create the connection that lasts forever.

I'm Just Like My ... Grandpa

❤ Do you have a cleft chin?

....
....
....
....
....
....
....

❤ Is your chin pointed or round?

....
....
....
....
....
....
....

❤ **Do you have a unibrow?**

....
....
....
....
....
....
....

❤ **Do you have long or short eyelashes?**

....
....
....
....
....
....
....

Create the connection that lasts forever.

I'm Just Like My ... Grandpa

If you can't do anything else to help along, just smile.

~ Eleanor Kirk

❤ **Do you squint when you smile?**

....
....
....
....
....
....
....

❤ **Do you have a heavy or light beard?**

....
....
....
....
....
....
....

❤ **Do you have thick or thin ankles?**

....
....
....
....
....
....
....

❤ **Do you have thick or thin wrists?**

....
....
....
....
....
....
....

Create the connection that lasts forever.

I'm Just Like My ... Grandpa

The average height for American men today is 5'7".

❤ **How tall are you?**

....

....

....

....

....

....

....

❤ **Do you have long legs or short legs?**

....

....

....

....

....

....

❤ Do you have lots of hair on your body or just a little?

....
....
....
....
....
....

Men lose about 40 hairs a day. Women lose about 70 hairs a day.

❤ Are you high-waisted or low-waisted?

....
....
....
....
....
....

Create the connection that lasts forever.

❤ **Do you have an "inny" or "outy" belly button?**

....

....

....

....

....

....

❤ **Do you have a long or short trunk?**

....

....

....

....

....

....

❤ Are your arms long, short or medium?

....

....

....

....

....

....

....

❤ Do you cross your arms right-over-left or left-over-right?

....

....

....

....

....

Create the connection that lasts forever.

I'm Just Like My ... Grandpa

❤ **What is your ring size?**

....

....

....

....

....

....

....

❤ **Are you allergic to anything?**

....

....

....

....

....

....

The following eight foods account for 90% of all food-allergic reactions: milk, egg, peanut and tree nuts (walnut, cashew, etc.), fish, shellfish, soy and wheat.

❤ Are you coordinated or clumsy?

....

....

....

....

....

....

....

❤ Is your skin smooth or rough?

....

....

....

....

....

....

Create the connection that lasts forever.

I'm Just Like My ... Grandpa

❤ Are your fingers and toes long or short?

....

....

....

....

....

....

❤ Do you have straight or curved thumbs?

....

....

....

....

....

....

❤ **Are your fingernails strong or weak?**

....

....

....

....

....

....

....

Fingernails grow nearly 4 times faster than toenails.

❤ **Do you bite your fingernails?**

....

....

....

....

....

....

....

Create the connection that lasts forever.

I'm Just Like My ... Grandpa

❤ **Are you right handed or left handed?**

....

....

....

....

....

....

....

International left-handers day is August 13.

❤ **Are your second toes longer than your big toes?**

....

....

....

....

....

....

❤ What is your shoe size?

....

....

....

....

....

....

....

❤ Are your feet wide or narrow?

....

....

....

....

....

....

Create the connection that lasts forever.

I'm Just Like My ... Grandpa

❤ **Do you have a deep voice or a high voice?**

....
....
....
....
....
....
....

❤ **Can you sing well?**

....
....
....
....
....
....
....

❤ **Can you whistle with just your lips?**

....

....

....

....

....

....

....

❤ **Can you whistle using your fingers?**

....

....

....

....

....

....

....

Create the connection that lasts forever.

I'm Just Like My ... Grandpa

❤ **Can you roll your Rs?**

....
....
....
....
....
....
....

❤ **Can you touch your tongue to your nose?**

....
....
....
....
....
....
....

Your tongue is the strongest muscle in your body.

❤ **Can you roll your tongue?**

....

....

....

....

....

....

....

Or are you even more special and have the ability to turn it into a "w"?

....

....

....

❤ **Can you wiggle your ears?**

....

....

....

....

....

....

Create the connection that lasts forever.

❤ **Can you wiggle your nose?**

....

....

....

....

....

....

....

❤ **Can you flare your nostrils?**

....

....

....

....

....

....

....

❤ Can you blow a bubble with gum?

....
....
....
....
....
....
....

According to Guinness World Records, the greatest diameter for a bubble gum bubble is 23".

❤ Do you have a unique physical characteristic?

....
....
....
....
....
....

Create the connection that lasts forever.

❤ Are you limber or stiff?

....

....

....

....

....

....

....

❤ Have you ever been able to do a cartwheel?

....

....

....

....

....

....

....

❤ Have you ever been able to do a hand stand?

....
....
....
....
....
....

❤ Can you bend over and touch your toes?

....
....
....
....
....
....

❤ **Do you sunburn or go directly to tan?**

....

....

....

....

....

....

❤ **What is your blood type?**

....

....

....

....

....

....

Section Two

❤ personal details & preferences

❤ **Are you energetic or calm?**

....

....

....

....

....

....

....

I'm Just Like My ... Grandpa

❤ **Are you a morning person or a night owl?**

....
....
....
....
....
....
....

❤ **Are you a deep sleeper or a light sleeper?**

....
....
....
....
....
....
....

❤ **What do you wear to sleep?**

....
....
....
....
....
....
....

❤ **What is your favorite sleeping position?**

....
....
....
....
....
....
....

I'm Just Like My ... Grandpa

❤ **Do you sleeps with one pillow or multiple pillows?**

Are your pillows soft or hard?

....

....

....

❤ **Do you like a soft or hard mattress?**

❤ **Do you fall asleep when your head hits the pillow or does it take awhile to doze off?**

....

....

....

....

....

....

The average person falls asleep in seven minutes.

❤ **Do you like to sleep in a cold room with lots of covers or a warm room with few covers?**

....

....

....

....

....

....

I'm Just Like My ... Grandpa

Scientists have found that it is impossible to tickle yourself. A region in the posterior portion of the brain, warns the rest of your brain when you are attempting to tickle yourself.

❤ **Where are you ticklish?**

....
....
....
....
....
....
....

❤ **Are you a leader or a follower?**

....
....
....
....
....
....
....

❤ **Do you have a nervous habit?**

....

....

....

....

....

....

....

❤ **What makes you laugh?**

....

....

....

....

....

....

Nothing is more significant of men's character than what they laugh at.
~ Johann von Goethe

❤ Are you a good speller?

....
....
....
....
....
....
....

❤ Do you prefer baths or showers?

....
....
....
....
....
....
....

Water consumption averages 7-10 gallons for showers, baths average 20 gallons.

❤ **What makes you cry?**

....

....

....

....

....

....

Tears are often the telescope through which men see far into heaven.
~ Henry Ward Beecher

❤ **Are you messy or neat?**

....

....

....

....

....

....

Create the connection that lasts forever.

I'm Just Like My ... Grandpa

Never fear shadows. They simply mean there's a light shining somewhere.

~ Ruth E. Renkel

❤ **What are you afraid of?**

....

....

....

....

....

....

❤ **What leg do you put into your pants first?**

....

....

....

....

....

....

❤ **What type of music do you prefer?**

....
....
....
....
....
....
....

❤ **Can you play a musical instrument?**

....

If so, did you ever take lessons on this instrument?

....
....

....

....

....

....

....

....

Create the connection that lasts forever.

I'm Just Like My ... Grandpa

According to Crayola®, America's favorite crayon color is blue.

❤ **What is your favorite color?**

....
....
....
....
....
....
....

❤ **What is your favorite holiday?**

....
....
....
....
....
....
....

❤ **What is your favorite weather?**

....
....
....
....
....
....
....

❤ **What is your favorite domestic animal?**

....
....
....
....
....
....
....

Create the connection that lasts forever.

I'm Just Like My ... Grandpa

❤ **What is your favorite wild animal?**

....

....

....

....

....

....

....

❤ **What is your favorite smell?**

....

....

....

....

....

....

....

How about bread baking or line-dried cotton sheets or freshly cut grass or pine trees or the smell after a rain or ...

❤ Are you an outdoor or an indoor person?

....

....

....

....

....

....

....

❤ What is your favorite season?

....

....

....

....

....

....

I'm Just Like My ... Grandpa

❤ **Would you rather vacation in a tent or a hotel?**

....

....

....

....

....

....

❤ **Do you prefer the mountains or the beach?**

....

....

....

....

....

....

He can climb the highest mountain or swim the biggest ocean. He can fly the fastest plane and fight the strongest tiger. My father can do anything! But most of the time he just carries out the garbage.

~ Anonymous 8-year-old

❤ **Do you prefer boxers or briefs?**

....

....

....

....

....

....

....

❤ **Do you like surprises?**

....

....

....

....

....

....

....

Create the connection that lasts forever.

❤ Can you keep a secret?

....

....

....

....

....

....

....

❤ Do you like being alone or with a group?

....

....

....

....

....

....

....

❤ Is your glass half empty or half full?

....

....

....

....

....

....

....

❤ Are you shy or outgoing?

....

....

....

....

....

....

....

Create the connection that lasts forever.

❤ **What kinds of snacks do you like?**

....
....
....
....
....
....
....

❤ **What is your favorite hot beverage?**

....
....
....
....
....
....
....

❤ What is your favorite cold beverage?

....

....

....

....

....

....

....

❤ Is your favorite meal breakfast, lunch or dinner?

....

....

....

....

....

Create the connection that lasts forever.

I'm Just Like My ... Grandpa

❤ **What do you like on your hamburgers?**

....

....

....

....

....

....

❤ **What is your favorite fruit?**

....

....

....

....

....

....

There are more than 100 varieties of bananas, some even have red skin.

❤ **What is your favorite vegetable?**

....

....

....

....

....

....

....

My husband thinks that health food is anything he eats before the expiration date.
~ Rita Rudner

❤ **What is your least favorite food?**

....

....

....

....

....

....

....

I'm Just Like My ... Grandpa

❤ **Do you like food hot & spicy or mild?**

....
....
....
....
....
....
....

❤ **What do you like on your pizza?**

Americans, on the average, eat 18 acres of pizza every day.

....
....
....
....
....
....
....

❤ **What is your favorite ice cream topping?**

....

....

....

....

....

....

....

❤ **What is your favorite sport to watch?**

....

....

....

....

....

....

....

Create the connection that lasts forever.

I'm Just Like My ... Grandpa

Sports serve society by providing vivid examples of excellence.

~ George F. Will

❤ **What is your favorite sport to play?**

....
....
....
....
....
....
....

❤ **Do you like to read?**

If you like to read, what types of books do you prefer?

....
....
....

....
....
....
....
....
....

❤ Are you creative or analytical?

....
....
....
....
....
....
....

❤ Can you swim?

....
....
....
....
....
....
....

Create the connection that lasts forever.

❤ Have you ever done a flip off a diving board?

....
....
....
....
....
....

❤ For what did you ever win a ribbon or a trophy?

....
....
....
....
....
....

❤ Do you talk to yourself out loud?

....

....

....

....

....

....

....

❤ In your family, are you the oldest, youngest, middle, in-between, or only child?

....

....

....

....

....

....

If you're in-between, where are you in the order?

....

....

....

Create the connection that lasts forever.

I'm Just Like My ... Grandpa

According to Fact Monster, these are the five most popular pet names: Max, Sam, Lady, Bear and Smokey.

❤ Do you have a favorite pet?

....
....
....
....
....
....

❤ Do you remember other people's names or faces best?

....
....
....
....
....

❤ **What was your favorite subject in school?**

....

....

....

....

....

....

....

Create the connection that lasts forever.

I'm Just Like My ... Grandpa

❤ **Use this space for anything else you may want to share.**

I'm Just Like My ...

❤ About the author

Vickie Mullins is the compassionate, driving force behind *I'm Just Like My ...*

Her professional writing passions run deep. She started her writing career with inspiration from a high school journalism class. Her writing talent and interest carried her through college and evolved into her founding of The Write Advantage, Inc., a full-service newsletter and business communications production company founded in 1991.

Growing up, Vickie was a tomboy, daughter of an avid hunter and fisherman. She loves hiking and the out-door lifestyle. Her idea of a perfect day is one spent fishing on the banks of any mountain lake. As it was for him, it is for her; **she is just like her dad**.

Vickie's personal passion is her family. She was inspired by her own mom to want to stay at home when her own children were born. So, her home-based business was born out of that vision. "Being a mom is the best job in the world," shares Vickie. She took one day at a time and tried to fill it with laughs and memories the kids would always cherish. **She is just like her mom**.

This is Vickie's first book. *I'm Just Like My ...* documents familial traits and tendencies in a loving and thoughtful manner for future family reference. Its subtitle, "Create the Connection That Lasts Forever," says it all.

You may be interested in submitting your story of how you're just like ... for upcoming books in the series. Please submit your tribute as a text file. Your submission serves as your written approval to publish. Send to the address below or email your text document to connect@imjustlikemy.com. Thank you.

Azure Eyes Publishing
7520 E. Second St., Suite 5
Scottsdale, Arizona 85251
(480) 941-8202
connect@ImJustLikeMy.com

Printed in the United States
36664LVS00002B/155-196